Instant JRebel

Accelerate your code development dramatically with this practical guide

Jonathan Lermitage

PUBLISHING

BIRMINGHAM - MUMBAI

Instant JRebel

First published: November 2013

Production Reference: 1221113

Published by Packt Publishing Ltd.
Livery Place
35 Livery Street
Birmingham B3 2PB, UK.

ISBN 978-1-84969-880-1

www.packtpub.com

Credits

Author
Jonathan Lermitage

Reviewers
Anton Arhipov
Viacheslav Dobromyslov
Nick Humphrey

Acquisition Editors
Owen Roberts
Erol Staveley

Commissioning Editor
Sruthi Kutty

Technical Editor
Amit Shetty

Project Coordinator
Joel Goveya

Proofreader
Clyde Jenkins

Production Coordinator
Shantanu Zagade

Cover Work
Shantanu Zagade

Cover Image
Nilesh Mohite

About the Author

Jonathan Lermitage, is a 29-year old programmer and French national. Jonathan has worked for five years with the Java SOA and BPM ecosystem, and the NetBeans IDE for a medium-sized company. Now, he is working for one of the European e-business leaders helping them to modernize and optimize their products. Also, he is trying to return to school in order to become an Engineer in Scientific Computing and Mathematics, his first passion and wish.

He has worked as a Technical Reviewer on *Instant NetBeans IDE How-to, Atul Palandurkar, Packt Publishing*.

Living with a computing fanatic is not easy every day, so I thank my parents, and my marvelous girlfriend for all their patience and encouragements.

About the Reviewers

Anton Arhipov is a Software Engineer and JRebel Product Manager at ZeroTurnaround, responsible for product features and roadmap. His professional interests include programming languages, middleware, and tooling. He is a Java enthusiast, vim fan, and an IntelliJ IDEA addict. He is also a JetBrains Academy member.

ZeroTurnaround, creator of JRebel and LiveRebel, is committed to making Java technology more productive by building innovative productivity tools for development teams.

Viacheslav Dobromyslov is a System Architect who spends most of his time projecting and developing enterprise accounting and international online trading systems with Java, PHP, and JavaScript. He has a degree in Computer Science and Engineering from the Far Eastern Federal University. He lives in the Far East Russia in the suburb of Vladivostok. He works on international projects and established good partnership relations with overseas companies from Japan, China, Australia, and New Zealand.

Nick Humphrey lives in Norway, and currently works as a Senior Developer in Java, Linux, and web technologies, developing and maintaining the Norwegian grocery industry's transportation ordering system, TakeCargo. Nick holds a Bachelor of Information Technology degree from NITH, Oslo, Norway.

In his free time, he composes and produces music using open source music technologies on Ubuntu Linux, under the artist name "Nickleus".

I'd like to personally thank the open source Internet community in general for all the help I've received in solving diverse, technological challenges over the years.

www.PacktPub.com

Support files, eBooks, discount offers and more

You might want to visit www.PacktPub.com for support files and downloads related to your book.

Did you know that Packt offers eBook versions of every book published, with PDF and ePub files available? You can upgrade to the eBook version at www.PacktPub.com and as a print book customer, you are entitled to a discount on the eBook copy. Get in touch with us at service@packtpub.com for more details.

At www.PacktPub.com, you can also read a collection of free technical articles, sign up for a range of free newsletters and receive exclusive discounts and offers on Packt books and eBooks.

http://PacktLib.PacktPub.com

Do you need instant solutions to your IT questions? PacktLib is Packt's online digital book library. Here, you can access, read and search across Packt's entire library of books.

Why Subscribe?

- ▸ Fully searchable across every book published by Packt
- ▸ Copy and paste, print and bookmark content
- ▸ On demand and accessible via web browser

Free Access for Packt account holders

If you have an account with Packt at www.PacktPub.com, you can use this to access PacktLib today and view nine entirely free books. Simply use your login credentials for immediate access.

Table of Contents

Preface

Software development takes time, and consists of many phases. Meanwhile, two phases (software compilation and deployment) are ignored because they take a lot of time. Recompiling a large application is usually too long, and some users prefer to use a continuous-integration server, such as Hudson or Jenkins. It is a good idea, but you still have to wait to test and validate your work. This problem exists for both desktop and web applications. Also, web applications have to be deployed and updated after each code change, which is time consuming.

Modern IDEs are able to improve the compilation and deployment steps. Actually, they already do a very good job, and you could think it is not possible to work even faster. This is the main objective of this book. JRebel does the same job as IDEs, but you will understand why it is a killer app. Compilation and deployment times are almost reduced to zero.

What this book covers

Introducing JRebel (Must know) shows the principle of class loaders and how to improve their usage with IDE's smart-build systems and JRebel. Also, it explains why you should prefer JRebel.

Registerting a JRebel account (Must know) explains how to register a free account in order to use JRebel. This technology is not free, but most programmers may be able to get a license at no cost or a trial.

JRebel for a standalone Tomcat server (Should know) helps you to understand how easily we can integrate the JRebel technology with Apache Tomcat standalone server.

JRebel for a standalone GlassFish server (Should know) explains how to install and activate JRebel on GlassFish standalone server.

JRebel plugin for IDEs (Must know) explains how to install the JRebel plugin in three major IDEs: Eclipse, IntelliJ IDEA, and NetBeans. Also, you will see how to activate your JRebel license to use it with your IDE.

Working with Java SE projects (Should know) demonstrates the power of JRebel by using this technology with classical desktop applications; typically, software with a Swing graphical interface. Please note it also works with console applications.

Working with Java EE projects (Must know) explains probably the most interesting usage of JRebel. In this recipe, you will deploy a very simple servlet-based web application and learn how to accelerate your development dramatically.

Discovering LiveRebel (Become an expert) gives some words about popular frameworks support such as Hibernate and Spring. Also, it talks about best companion of JRebel; that is, LiveRebel, designed for production environments. Finally, you will be introduced to the JRebel license server, useful for large companies.

What you need for this book

You need to install a JDK (prefer Version 7), your favourite IDE: Eclipse, IntelliJ IDEA, or NetBeans. Also, you will need to download and install the latest version of Tomcat and Glassfish.

Who this book is for

The target audience of this book consists of people who know the Java SE and Java EE applications, but they need not be experts. Actually, simple Hello World programs can be connected with JRebel. Also, this is for audiences who know to use an IDE and how to install and configure it. They will understand how to accelerate their development with JRebel.

Conventions

In this book, you will find a number of styles of text that distinguish between different kinds of information. Here are some examples of these styles, and an explanation of their meaning.

Code words in text are shown as follows: "You will be redirected to the jButton1ActionPerformed method of your JFrame object."

A block of code is set as follows:

```
private void jButton1ActionPerformed
  (java.awt.event.ActionEvent evt) {
  // TODO add your handling code here:
  // jLabel1.setText("Hello World"); // previous message
  jLabel1.setText("Hello Planet");   // new message
}
```

Any command-line input or output is written as follows:

```
-Drebel.remoting_plugin=true
```

New terms and **important words** are shown in bold. Words that you see on the screen, in menus or dialog boxes, for example, appear in the text like this: "Simply don't forget to enable the **Use IDE's proxy settings** feature."

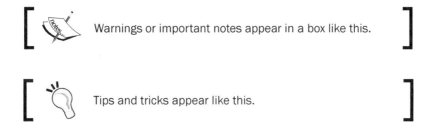

Warnings or important notes appear in a box like this.

Tips and tricks appear like this.

Reader feedback

Feedback from our readers is always welcome. Let us know what you think about this book—what you liked or may have disliked. Reader feedback is important for us to develop titles that you really get the most out of.

To send us general feedback, simply send an e-mail to feedback@packtpub.com, and mention the book title via the subject of your message.

If there is a topic that you have expertise in and you are interested in either writing or contributing to a book, see our author guide on www.packtpub.com/authors.

Customer support

Now that you are the proud owner of a Packt book, we have a number of things to help you to get the most from your purchase.

Downloading the example code

You can download the example code files for all Packt books you have purchased from your account at http://www.packtpub.com. If you purchased this book elsewhere, you can visit http://www.packtpub.com/support and register to have the files e-mailed directly to you.

Errata

Although we have taken every care to ensure the accuracy of our content, mistakes do happen. If you find a mistake in one of our books—maybe a mistake in the text or the code—we would be grateful if you would report this to us. By doing so, you can save other readers from frustration and help us improve subsequent versions of this book. If you find any errata, please report them by visiting `http://www.packtpub.com/submit-errata`, selecting your book, clicking on the **errata submission form** link, and entering the details of your errata. Once your errata are verified, your submission will be accepted and the errata will be uploaded on our website, or added to any list of existing errata, under the Errata section of that title. Any existing errata can be viewed by selecting your title from `http://www.packtpub.com/support`.

Piracy

Piracy of copyright material on the Internet is an ongoing problem across all media. At Packt, we take the protection of our copyright and licenses very seriously. If you come across any illegal copies of our works, in any form, on the Internet, please provide us with the location address or website name immediately so that we can pursue a remedy.

Please contact us at `copyright@packtpub.com` with a link to the suspected pirated material.

We appreciate your help in protecting our authors, and our ability to bring you valuable content.

Questions

You can contact us at `questions@packtpub.com` if you are having a problem with any aspect of the book, and we will do our best to address it.

Instant JRebel

Welcome to *Instant JRebel*. This book is for Java developers who are not aware of JRebel technology and the improvement of deployment time.

Most programmers face long compilation times on large projects. This is also a problem when a web application has to be restarted to apply some changes. Most development environments provide tools to reduce these delays, but JRebel is probably the most innovative way to handle large projects. You will learn how to integrate this technology into your current and future projects: Java SE and EE projects on local and remote servers, with any IDE.

Introducing JRebel (Must know)

Before trying to use JRebel, let's have a look at the existing features offered by modern IDEs such as NetBeans. They are already able to accelerate your developments. We will see later why JRebel is a better choice.

Also, many developers associate JRebel with Java EE applications only, but keep in mind it works with any Java SE application too, including GUI software!

How to do it...

Modern IDEs offer some ways to accelerate your developments and deployments. We will show one of them, called **Deploy on Save** on NetBeans using the following steps:

1. Understand what a class loader is. Download and install the latest version of Oracle JDK7 from `http://www.oracle.com/technetwork/java/javase/downloads/index.html` (on Ubuntu, you may use `the sudo apt-get install openjdk-7-jdk` command to install JDK7) and NetBeans IDE from `https://netbeans.org/downloads/`. Please choose the **Java EE** or **All** bundle of NetBeans.

2. Download and install the latest binary version of Apache Tomcat server from `http://tomcat.apache.org/download-70.cgi`. You should use the ZIP version. It is easier to register in NetBeans than the Windows Service Installer version.

3. Register the Tomcat server in NetBeans by launching NetBeans and going to the **Services** tab. Right-click on the **Servers** node, then click on the **Add Server...** register, then choose **Apache Tomcat** from the server list to register the Tomcat server.

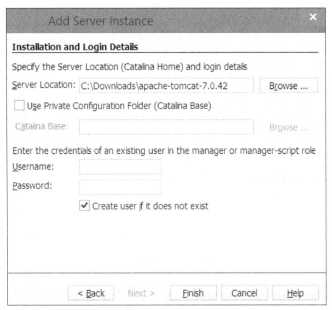

Registering Tomcat into NetBeans

4. Create a simple Java web project. You can do it by navigating to **File | New Project | Java Web | Web Application**. Remember to choose Tomcat as the server. It will create a simple web application with a HelloWorld JSP file. Now, create a simple servlet by navigating to **File | New File | Web | Servlet**. See the differences when **Compile on Save** is enabled and disabled. You can activate this feature present in the **Projects Properties** panel by checking the **Deploy on Save** checkbox.

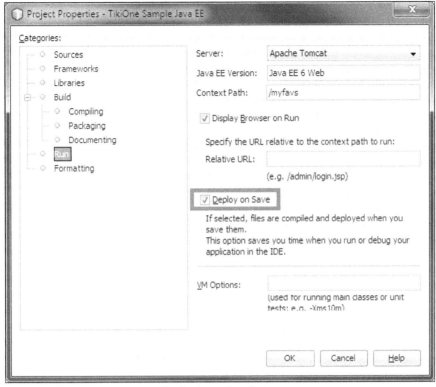

The Deploy on Save feature

How it works...

A web application is a good example to explain the principle of the **Deploy on Save** feature of NetBeans.

You probably already know that you can modify and save a JSP file; the server will automatically reload it without restarting or redeploying anything. Meanwhile, servlets are Java classes and won't be reloaded so easily. Without the help from an IDE, you would normally need to rebuild your application and redeploy it.

The **Deploy on Save** feature is designed to redeploy your servlets automatically. You only have to save the edited file and you'll see the changes immediately.

So, is there anything else to improve the development process?

Unfortunately, the **Deploy on Save** system is limited it consumes time and can't update the entire web applications or configuration files. This is exactly why JRebel is useful. JRebel is comparable to the best **Deploy on Save** systems, but it also offers many advanced capabilities. It offers two types of improvements:

▶ Changes to Class structure: This targets Java SE applications (such as desktop applications) and Java EE applications.

▶ JRebel is able to apply changes to many Java elements. The following are the details:

  ❑ It applies changes to method bodies
  ❑ It adds/removes methods
  ❑ It adds/removes constructors
  ❑ It adds/removes fields
  ❑ It adds/removes annotations
  ❑ It adds/removes classes
  ❑ It applies changes to static field values
  ❑ It adds/removes enumeration values
  ❑ It applies changes to interfaces

▶ Instant Builds: It targets Java EE applications only. JRebel is able to apply changes to Java EE elements. The following are the details:

  ❑ It skips builds for WAR directories
  ❑ It skips builds for WAR/EAR class updates
  ❑ It skips builds for WAR/EAR resource updates
  ❑ It maps multiple source dirs to one WAR/EAR target dir
  ❑ It maps classes and resources with include/exclude patterns
  ❑ It maps multiple source dirs with Ant-style patterns
  ❑ It uses system properties to make mapping machine-independent

JRebel is entirely transparent; simply save the modifications to observe changes in the live application. It works with any kind of Java application.

Registering a JRebel account (Must know)

To use JRebel, you need a **ZeroTurnaround** account. We'll see how to register a trial account for commercial projects and a free account for open source and non-commercial development.

Getting ready

You can register two types of accounts: a free account for open source or Scala projects, or a 14-day trial (for commercial purposes).

Also, free accounts don't allow you to integrate JRebel in a standalone server, you'll have to use the JRebel plugin for IDEs. In other words, it means that a free account allows you to register a server in the IDE and use the JRebel plugin only; you always work on your local machine. The trial version doesn't have this limitation and allows you to install JRebel directly in a server; this way you can use a server installed on a remote machine, and use NetBeans and its JRebel plugin to connect to the remote server.

To get a free account, go to `https://my.jrebel.com/register` and fill out the form to register an account. You can also use your Facebook or Twitter account, but keep in mind ZeroTurnaround will ask you about posting contents on your behalf. You will receive a confirmation e-mail. Once your account is confirmed, return to the previous link and use your new account to log in (if needed). Now, you have to choose one of the three available plans. Go to `https://my.jrebel.com/plans` and choose a plan from the following:

- **Scala**: This plan is used for Scala projects
- **OSS**: This plan is used for open source software
- **Social**: This means that you will connect your Facebook or Twitter account to your JRebel account

 Keep in mind that these three plans are for non-commercial projects only, otherwise, please use the 14-day trial. ZeroTurnaround, the creator of JRebel, is able to invalidate your license without notice, remotely.

Complete the forms and you will receive a license key by e-mail. You can also visit `https://my.jrebel.com/account/how-to-activate` to get it immediately.

To get a trial license, go to `http://zeroturnaround.com/software/jrebel/trial/` and fill out the form on right-hand of the web page to register a 14-day trial account. Once registered, you will be automatically redirected to a web page that shows your JRebel Product Activation Key. Copy it in a text editor, we will be using it very soon. You will also receive an e-mail from `zeroturnaround.com` containing this key.

If you have already tested JRebel with a free trial account, you may want to use it in a commercial project. To buy a commercial license, visit `http://zeroturnaround.com/software/jrebel/buy/` and choose the **Base** or **Enterprise** option. The main difference between these two plans is the number of developers in your company. Also, enterprise licenses come with a license server, a tool that gives you more control of your license files (you can easily activate and revoke licenses). Check `http://zeroturnaround.com/software/jrebel/download/license-server/` for more details.

How to do it...

In this section, we will see how to register and activate your JRebel license. The following are the steps to register and activate it:

1. Download the JRebel runtime from `http://zeroturnaround.com/software/jrebel/download/#!/`. The download link is at the bottom of the page: please use the «current stable» version of JRebel), and extract it to your local drive. In this tutorial, we will assume that JRebel has been unpacked to `C:\packtpub\jrebel\`.

2. Run `C:\packtpub\jrebel\bin\jrebel-config.cmd` (or the corresponding `*.sh` script file, if you are using a Linux operating system).

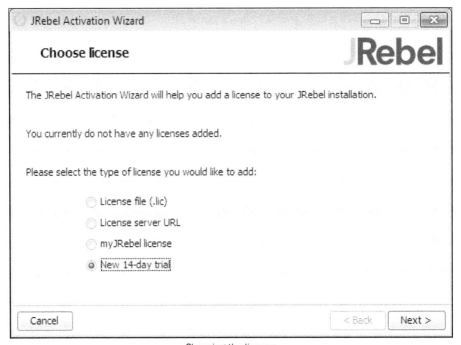

Choosing the license

3. Choose the **New 14-day trial** option if you have registered a 14-day trial account. Otherwise, choose the **myJRebel license** option.

4. Validate the first screen and paste your license key.

Copy/paste the license key

5. Validate the screen. You'll see the following message: **JRebel has been successfully activated, thank you!**. Close the wizard; your JRebel license is now activated.

License validation

6. To finish, go to the user profile directory of your operating system, in the `.jrebel` subdirectory (`%userprofile%\.jrebel\` on MS Windows); you will see a `jrebel.lic` file that contains your (encrypted) license key. This is the file that JRebel will check at every startup.

JRebel for a standalone Tomcat server (Should know)

We'll see how to install and activate JRebel on a Tomcat standalone server.

How to do it...

The following are the steps that describe how to activate JRebel on a Tomcat server:

1. Download and unzip the Tomcat server.

2. Launch Tomcat with the startup script located in its `bin` directory (`bin\startup.bat` on MS Windows).

3. Enable the **JRebel Java Agent** for the Tomcat server. To proceed, simply append `-javaagent:C:\packtpub\jrebel\jrebel.jar` to the `JAVA_OPTS` environment variable.

How it works...

To proceed, you will need the latest version of Tomcat 6 or Tomcat 7, a Java 6 (or Java 7) JRE or JDK, and a trial (or commercial) activated license. Free licenses don't allow you to run JRebel on standalone servers!

Once installed and configured, add the JRebel Java Agent to the startup parameters of Tomcat.

Tomcat is now configured to launch the JRebel Java Agent.

Launch Tomcat with the startup script and look at the console output or Tomcat logs. If JRebel is correctly launched, you will see messages that indicate your JRebel license is active. Otherwise, you have probably forgotten to register your license, or you have misspelled the JRebel Java Agent path.

The following is an example of the normal JRebel activation, with message displayed in Tomcat's default output:

JRebel: JRebel 5.3.1 (201307011846)

JRebel: (c) Copyright ZeroTurnaround OU, Estonia, Tartu.

JRebel:

JRebel: Over the last 1 days JRebel prevented

JRebel: at least 0 redeploys/restarts saving you about 0 hours.

JRebel:

JRebel: You are running with an evaluation license.

JRebel: You have 14 days until the license expires.

JRebel:

JRebel: You will see this notification until you obtain a

JRebel: full license for your installation.

Please note that Tomcat will display timestamps in its default output and logs. They have been removed from this example for visibility purposes.

JRebel for a standalone GlassFish server (Should know)

We'll see how to install and activate JRebel on GlassFish standalone server.

How to do it...

The following are the steps that describe how to activate JRebel on GlassFish server:

1. Download and GlassFish server from `https://glassfish.java.net/download.html` and unzip it.

2. Launch GlassFish with the startup script located in its `bin` folder (`bin\asadmin.bat` on MS Windows). To start the default domain, run this command: `asadmin start-domain domain1`.

3. Enable the JRebel Java Agent for the GlassFish server. To proceed, launch your favorite Internet browser and visit `http://localhost:4848/`, you will be connected to the administration interface of GlassFish. Navigate to **Configurations | server-config | JVM-settings** in the left-side panel.

4. Add the two JVM options: `javaagent:C:\packtpub\jrebel\jrebel.jar` and `-Drebel.log=true`.

How it works...

To proceed, you will need the latest version of GlassFish 3 (or GlassFish 4), and a Java 6 (or Java 7) JDK. Once installed and configured, launch GlassFish with its startup script I.

Launch your favorite Internet browser and visit `http://localhost:4848/`.

Now, add two JVM options as displayed on the following screenshot:

► `-javaagent:C:\packtpub\jrebel\jrebel.jar`

► `-Drebel.log=true`

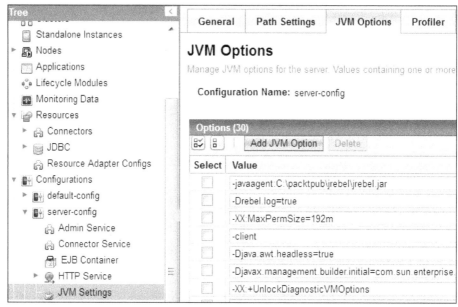

Setting JVM options in GlassFish

You already know the first JVM option, this is the JRebel Java Agent.

The second JVM option asks JRebel to enable its logs. These logs will contain information about your current license validity, and so on. We have to turn on this option because GlassFish won't write JRebel logs to the default output. So, without JRebel logs, you could not know If JRebel is correctly loaded by GlassFish.

When you have added the two JVM options and validated the corresponding form, shut down your GlassFish server with the `asadmin stop-domain domain1` command. After that, start your server again and check the `C:\Packtpub\jrebel\jrebel.log` file. It will contain a lot of information, including the message that indicates your license is active.

Now, please note that you don't need the `-Drebel.log=true` JVM option anymore; we used it to check JRebel configuration only. You can edit the GlassFish JVM option list and remove it. Re-enable it only if you encounter problems with JRebel.

Congratulations, your server is now configured to run JRebel!

JRebel plugin for IDEs (Must know)

The JRebel technology can be integrated in many IDEs, like Eclipse, IntelliJ IDEA, and NetBeans. We'll see how to install and activate the JRebel plugin on each platform.

Getting ready

You need to download and install at least one of these IDEs: Eclipse, IntelliJ IDEA, or NetBeans, and perform the following steps:

1. Download and install the latest version of **Eclipse IDE for Java EE Developers** from `http://www.eclipse.org/downloads/`. Please note that JRebel works on **Eclipse IDE for Java Developers** and **Eclipse Standard** editions too. Also, distributions delivered by Linux package managers (from Ubuntu, and so on) may work correctly. Once downloaded and installed, run it.

2. In this section, we will use the free version of **IntelliJ IDEA Community Edition**. If you have a commercial license for **IntelliJ IDEA Ultimate Edition**, you can use it. Download and install the latest version of IntelliJ IDEA Community Edition from `http://www.jetbrains.com/idea/download/`.

3. Download and install the latest version of NetBeans from `https://netbeans.org/downloads/`. Since the rest of this book will use NetBeans as its main IDE for Java SE and Java EE example projects, it is preferable to download the Java EE or All version.

How to do it...

The following steps will help you to integrate the JRebel plugin into your favorite IDE:

1. Download the JRebel plugin for IDE.
2. Activate your JRebel license in the IDE.

How it works...

In Eclipse, go to the menu toolbar and navigate to **Help | Eclipse Marketplace**. If you are lucky, you should already see the JRebel plugin listed in the **Eclipse Marketplace** window. Otherwise, simply search for JRebel and install it.

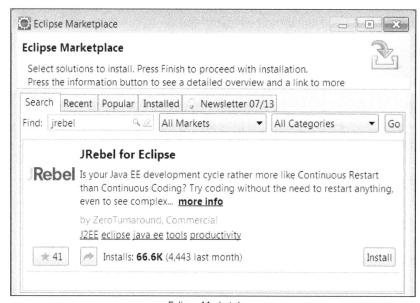

Eclipse Marketplace

Eclipse will ask you what components to install. Choose them all and validate.

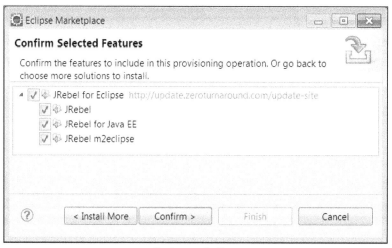

Features selection

Accept the JRebel license and validate again. Eclipse will now download the JRebel plugin.

Once downloaded, please restart Eclipse in order to complete the JRebel plugin installation.

To check the JRebel installation, go into the Eclipse preferences and type `JRebel` in the search box; you will see a JRebel section.

To finish, we need to activate the JRebel license, or simply check its status. To proceed, return to the Eclipse preferences, go to the JRebel section, and accept to open **JRebel Config Center**.

If you have already registered a license (as described in the *How to do it...* section of the *Registering a JRebel account (Must know)* recipe), you should see an activated license in the **Licensing** panel.

Licensing the information

Otherwise, use the **Activate / Update License** link, paste your license key and validate; your Eclipse JRebel plugin is now correctly installed and activated.

Also, please note this screen is useful to renew your license.

In IntelliJ IDEA, navigate to the **File** | **Settings** menu, and go to the **Plugins** section. Use the **Browse repositories...** button and search for JRebel. The full name of the plugin is **JRebel Plugin Tools Integration**. Download it.

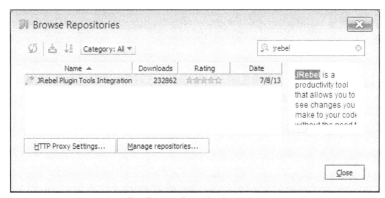

The Browse Repositories menu

Once downloaded, please restart IntelliJ IDEA in order to complete the JRebel plugin installation.

To check the JRebel installation, return into IntelliJ IDEA **Settings** and type `jrebel` in the search box; you will see a **JRebel** section.

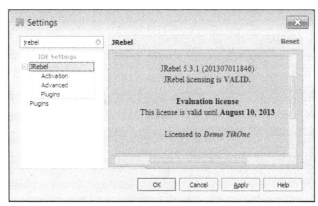

The Settings menu

To finish, use this screen to check your JRebel license activation. If needed, use the **Activation** panel to paste and register your license key.

Your IntelliJ IDEA JRebel plugin is now correctly installed and activated.

Also, please note that this screen is useful to renew your license.

In NetBeans, navigate to **Tools | Plugins | Available Plugins**, and search for JRebel.

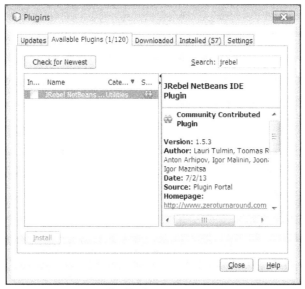

The Plugins manager

Download the plugin, accept the license, accept the JRebel self-signed certificate, and install the plugin. Once done, restart NetBeans.

To check the JRebel installation, navigate to **Tools | Options**, and open the **JRebel** panel.

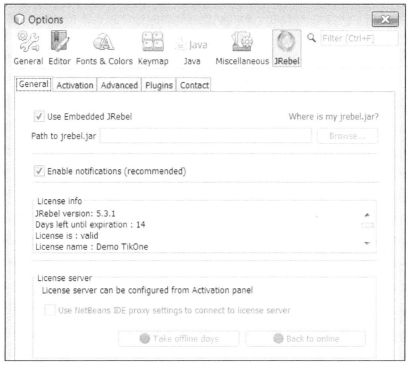

The JRebel panel

In the **General** tab of the **JRebel** panel, you can check the **License info** field. If your license is not activated, you can open the **Activation** tab to register your license key.

Your NetBeans JRebel plugin is now correctly installed and activated.

Also, please note that this screen is useful to renew your license.

There's more...

Now, let's talk about NetBeans special case.

We will now see how to download and install the JRebel plugin manually. There is one reason to proceed this way; every NetBeans plugin displayed in the **Plugins** manager has been validated by a verification team. If a plugin validation fails (for quality reasons), it may temporarily disappear from the **Plugins** manager. That's why you should know how to download the plugin manually.

To proceed, go to `http://plugins.netbeans.org/plugin/22254/`. This is the download page of the JRebel plugin for NetBeans. Choose the plugin version corresponding to your NetBeans version and download it—this is an NBM (NetBeans Module) file.

The NetBeans Plugins website

The **UC** badges indicate the plugin that has been validated and is available in the NetBeans integrated **Plugins** manager.

Now, return to NetBeans and navigate to **Tools** | **Plugins** | **Downloaded**, and use the **Add Plugins...** button to select the NBM file you have just downloaded. You can now install the plugin into NetBeans from this file.

This method is also a good way to install a new version of the JRebel plugin that has not been validated yet (plugins are usually validated after one week).

Working with Java SE projects (Should know)

We'll see how to work with JRebel on the Ant Java SE projects: a simple graphical application will be built and modified without any additional compilation, thanks to the JRebel live code injection. You will also get some words about Maven Java SE projects support. NetBeans will be used as the main IDE.

How to do it...

The following steps will show you how to experiment with JRebel on a Java SE application:

1. Create a simple Swing application and test it.

2. Enable JRebel on your project.

3. Try live code injection with JRebel.

How it works...

We will create a simple Swing application, a frame that contains a label and a button. The action associated with the button will update the label. We will use JRebel to change the button's action without recompiling or restarting the application.

Start NetBeans and create a new Java application project. Create a package, delete the default main class, and use the NetBeans assistant to create a new JFrame object by navigating to **File | New File | Swing GUI Forms | JFrame Form**, and then choose a name and validate.

The Projects view

Use the **Palette** tab on your right to drag-and-drop a **JLabel** and a **JButton** to your **JForm** (these two components are located in the **Swing Controls** section, under the **Label** and **Button** names).

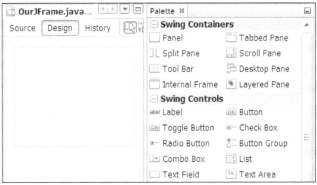

The Palette tab

Now, double-click on the button you have generated. You will be redirected to the `jButton1ActionPerformed` method of your JFrame object.

```
private void jButton1ActionPerformed
    (java.awt.event.ActionEvent evt) {
    // TODO add your handling code here:
}
```

Insert a code to update JLabel of your form, as shown in the following code:

```
private void jButton1ActionPerformed
    (java.awt.event.ActionEvent evt) {
    // TODO add your handling code here:
    jLabel1.setText("Hello World");
}
```

The application is now ready for testing. You can test it by pressing *F6* key. NetBeans will ask you for the name of the main class. Select the JFrame form and validate. Use the **jButton1** button to update the label.

The first Hello World window

Do not close the application immediately, and return to the code editor to update the **jButton1** button's action in order to display a new message and save the new code.

```
private void jButton1ActionPerformed
    (java.awt.event.ActionEvent evt) {
    // TODO add your handling code here:
    // jLabel1.setText("Hello World"); // previous message
    jLabel1.setText("Hello Planet");   // new message
}
```

Downloading the example code

You can download the example code files for all Packt books you have purchased from your account at http://www.packtpub. com. If you purchased this book elsewhere, you can visit http://www.packtpub.com/support and register to have the files e-mailed directly to you

Hit the **jButton1** button in your application again; the change is not effective. Actually, your application hasn't been updated and it can't reflect code changes immediately. You will have to restart your application to see the new behavior, and this is normal. Now, let's see how JRebel will accelerate the development.

You may have noticed the presence of a JRebel node in the **Projects** view. Right-click on it and choose **Generate rebel.xml**.

The JRebel XML

The `rebel.xml` file will contain the path of the compiled classes. JRebel will use these compiled classes to update your running application. Also, that means we have to ensure the **Compile on Save** feature is turned on for your project. Every time you apply changes to a Java class, NetBeans will recompile it and JRebel will update your running application with it. To proceed, go to the **Projects Properties** panel and enable the **Compile on Save** feature.

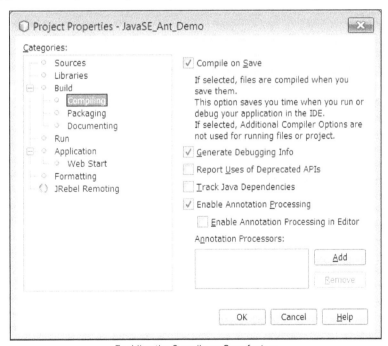

Enabling the Compile on Save feature

To finish, you have to activate JRebel (locate the JRebel button on the NetBeans toolbar).

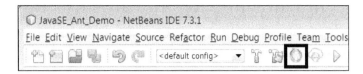

Enabling the JRebel button

Now, restart your application and hit the **jButton1** button a first time. Return to the code editor, modify the button's action to display a new message, save, and carefully observe the NetBeans console; you will see two interesting messages:

- ▸ Firstly, JRebel indicates if your license is active
- ▸ Secondly, you can see a message that indicates a class which has been reloaded, as follows:

  ```
  2013-07-28 15:08:03 JRebel: Reloading class 'demo.ant.OurJFrame'.

  2013-07-28 15:08:03 JRebel: Reloading class 'demo.ant.
  OurJFrame$2'.

  2013-07-28 15:08:03 JRebel: Reloading class 'demo.ant.
  OurJFrame$1'.
  ```

Hit the **jButton1** button again; the message changes without restarting the application. It works! You can now continue to update and save code in order to see the changes. Try to update the displayed message again, it works again; you don't need to restart your application again (except for some changes that are not supported by JRebel).

There's more...

Ant is not the only build system, so you may want to use JRebel with Maven-based projects.

Maven- and Ant-based projects are handled the same way: generate a `rebel.xml` file, activate the **Compile on Save** feature, enable JRebel, and simply update your code without restarting your application. You don't have to deal with the Maven `pom.xml` file.

Also, you will still see the two same JRebel messages in the NetBeans console. They are useful to check the JRebel license and class reloading.

Last but not least, to activate the **Compile On Save** feature, the **Compile On Save** menu should be set to **For application execution only** (or better).

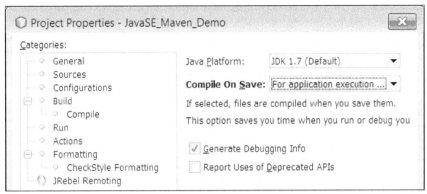

Maven's Compile On Save feature

Working with Java EE projects (Must know)

We'll see how to work with JRebel on Ant-based Java EE projects: a simple web application will be built and modified without any additional compilation. Also, two cases will be explained: when the server is on the development machine and managed by the IDE, and when the server is running on a remote machine. NetBeans will be used as the main IDE. Please note that Ant-based means that the NetBeans uses Ant to handle the project (such as the classical Java SE Ant-based project); we won't use Ant inside the application itself.

How to do it...

The following steps will help you to test the live code injection in a Java EE project:

1. Register the GlassFish local server in NetBeans.
2. Create a simple Java EE servlet-based project.
3. Enable JRebel on your project.
4. Try the live code injection with JRebel.

How it works...

First, register GlassFish in NetBeans (you can use the same GlassFish server that you have installed in the *JRebel for standalone GlassFish server (Should know)* recipe). To proceed, go to the **Services** panel and right-click on the **Servers** node.

Registering GlassFish

Select **Add Server...**, choose **GlassFish Server**, locate your GlassFish server-base installation directory, and validate with the **Next** button.

Locating GlassFish

Choose the **Register Local Domain** option and validate. Your GlassFish server is now registered into NetBeans.

To enable JRebel on GlassFish, you have the following two options:

  ▶ As described in the *JRebel for standalone GlassFish server (Should know)* recipe, you have already added the JRebel Java Agent as a startup parameter. It will automatically enable JRebel on your server.

▶ If you haven't added the JRebel Java Agent to the startup parameters, don't worry, the JRebel plugin can automatically add this Java Agent to any server that is registered in NetBeans. You simply have to check that the JRebel button in the NetBeans toolbar is turned on, and—this is very important—check that the **Use IDE's proxy settings** feature is activated in the **Servers** settings. To verify this last point, right-click on the registered server and show its **Properties** panel. Make sure that the **Use IDE's proxy settings** feature in checked.

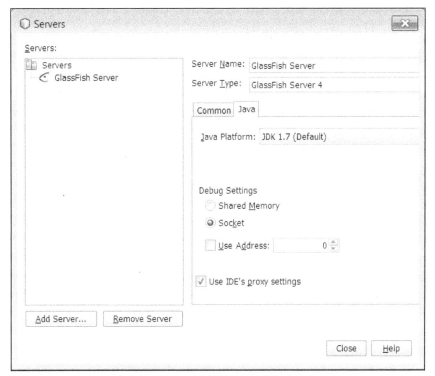

Activating the Use IDE's Proxy Settings feature

 Without the **Use IDE's proxy settings** feature, NetBeans won't be able to know that JRebel wants to add a parameter (its Java Agent) to the list of startup parameters of the registered server. This is valid for all registered servers: GlassFish, Tomcat, and so on.

Right-click on the registered server and start it. Observe the NetBeans console; you will see a message that indicates JRebel is activated on your server.

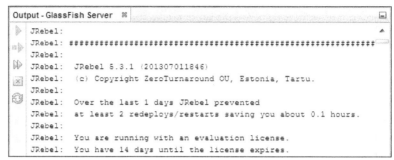

The NetBeans console and registered GlassFish

Now, create a new Ant-based web application project by navigating to **File | New Project | Java Web | Web Application**. Choose a name, select the registered GlassFish server and a Java EE version (version doesn't matter), and click on the **Finish** button.

Delete the default `index.html` (or `index.jsp`) file located in the **Web Pages** section, displayed in the **Projects** panel.

Create a package and use the NetBeans assistant to generate a servlet. This can be done by navigating to **File | New File | Web | Servlet**. Give it a name and click on the **Next** button. At the **Configure Servlet Deployment** step, fill the **Servlet Name** and **URL Pattern(s)** field.

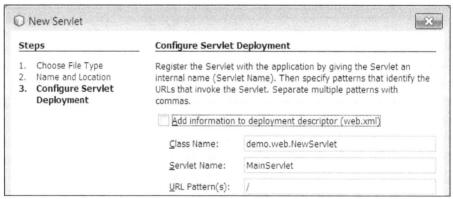

Configuring the servlet deployment properties

Similar to Java SE projects in the *Working with Java SE projects (Should know)* recipe, you have to generate a `rebel.xml` file. Go to the **Projects** panel, and use the **JRebel** node to generate this file.

You have to check the following two features in the **Projects Properties** panel:

▸ Enable the **Compile on Save** feature

Enabling the Compile on Save feature

▸ Disable the **Deploy on Save** feature

Disabling Deploy on Save feature

 The **Deploy on Save** and JRebel features are incompatible because they do the same thing: they try to update your web application without any restart. Since we want to use JRebel for its advanced capabilities, we have to disable the **Deploy on Save** feature. Actually, you can keep it enabled; you will see a warning message that indicates that these two features are incompatible and JRebel has been temporarily turned off.

To test JRebel with our web application, simply press the *F6* key. This will deploy your web application and start your web browser to show the main servlet.

We will assume your project is called `WebApplicationLocal`, and deployed at `http://localhost:8080/WebApplicationLocal`.

You will see a web page with the following message:

Servlet NewServlet at /WebApplicationLocal

This message is generated by the servlet which was created previously. We will now modify this message without restarting or redeploying anything. To proceed, open the `Servlet` class in the code editor, and go to the `processRequest` method. You will see the following line of code:

```
out.println("<h1>Servlet NewServlet at " +
    request.getContextPath() + "</h1>");
```

Modify it to display a new message, save it, and refresh only your web browser (do not redeploy); the message has been updated!

Look at the NetBeans console (as with Java SE projects), JRebel writes a message for each class that has been reloaded.

INFO: 2013-07-28 16:59:57 JRebel: Reloading class 'demo.web. NewServlet'.

Congratulations, you can now update your web application by simply saving changes in the code editor!

There's more...

We will see how to work with a remote Tomcat server and a simple servlet-based web application.

NetBeans is not able to register a remote Tomcat server but JRebel is. So, we will proceed this way: register a (dummy) local Tomcat in NetBeans and configure JRebel to work with the remote Tomcat server.

Registering a local Tomcat server in NetBeans

Register a local Tomcat server in NetBeans the same way you previously registered a local GlassFish server. This is the same assistant. Simply don't forget to enable the **Use IDE's proxy settings** feature.

Installing and configuring a remote Tomcat server

Also, install a Tomcat server on a remote computer (you can install it on your local machine for this tutorial; JRebel will simply warn you it is not a common scenario, but it will work fine). Don't forget to add the JRebel Java Agent to its list of startup parameters. In addition, there is another parameter to add, as follows:

-Drebel.remoting_plugin=true

This parameter will allow JRebel to receive new class definitions over the network.

Start the remote server. Compile your web application, upload it to your remote Tomcat server and deploy it via the Tomcat web administration interface. Note down its deployment context.

Configuring your project

When it is done, open your web application **Projects Properties** panel and do the following two things:

▸ Change the targeted server for Tomcat.

Changing the targeted server

▸ In the **JRebel Remoting** section, fill the **Application URL** field with your remote web application context (something like `http://yourserver:8080/WebApplicationLocal`, where "`yourserver`" is the name of your remote machine, "`8080`" is the communication port, and "`WebApplicationLocal`" is the context path of the web application). Also, click on the **Generate keys**, **Generate rebel.xml**, and **Generate rebel-remote.xml** buttons.

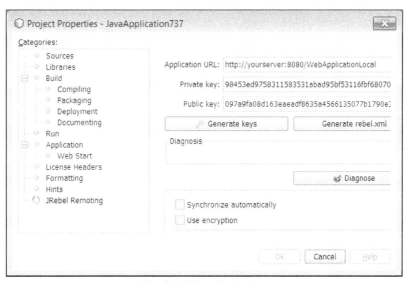

The JRebel Remoting section

Trying live code injection

You can now start modifying your application:

1. Modify a class in the code editor.
2. Save it (do not redeploy).
3. Press the JRebel synchronization button.

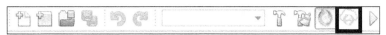

The JRebel synchronization button

Reload the remote webpage; its content has been updated!

Discovering LiveRebel (Become an expert)

JRebel is able to dramatically accelerate your developments, but it works for development phases only. You probably won't use JRebel with a production server. Of course, you could use an IDE, connect it to your production server, and use this system to keep your deployed applications up-to-date, but you would rapidly encounter problems—you have to use only one IDE to update your applications. This scenario is not suitable for a team of developers, and it is unprofessional.

An appropriate solution is LiveRebel. Since JRebel is ideal for the development stage, LiveRebel is designed to help you keep your production applications up-to-date, without any restart or redeployment.

LiveRebel is a link between your production environment and your continuous-integration server. More precisely, it is able to use your continuous-integration server to get the latest build and update your deployed application with it, live.

LiveRebel is very configurable and platform agnostic, which means it is not limited to Java! For details, please visit `http://zeroturnaround.com/software/liverebel/ what-we-support/#headline`. Also, note that LiveRebel comes with a free license that is valid for one year and works for two nodes (environments). LiveRebel commercial licenses are sold as annual licenses per JVM instance. You can get details by visiting `http://zeroturnaround.com/liverebel/pricing/`.

How to do it...

The following are the general steps on how to install LiveRebel and connect it to your environment:

1. These general steps will help you to prepare a testing environment and accelerate your deployments with LiveRebel. Set up a version-control system, such as Subversion, Mercurial, or Git.

2. Set up a continuous-integration server, such as TeamCity, Jenkins, Hudson, or Bamboo.

3. Set up your (pre)production application server and database (for example, Tomcat and MySQL).

4. Optionally, configure your favorite IDE to use your versioning system and continuous-integration server.

5. Visit `http://zeroturnaround.com/software/liverebel/` to get LiveRebel.

6. You will get the final download link by e-mail, with a license key. Download LiveRebel and unzip it.

7. Run the `bin/lr-command-center` script (BAT or SH, depending on your platform).

LiveRebel command center startup

8. Open the URL displayed in the console. To log in, please use information received by mail (with your license key). Create a user.

9. Use the **ADD SERVER** button to add your production application server, and follow the steps displayed in your Internet browser.

10. Use your IDE to modify code, commit to your versioning system and observe live changes on your production application.

How it works...

After code is committed or schedule, your continuous-integration server will release a new build, and LiveRebel will simply use it to update your production application, live.

This way, you neither have to install updates manually, nor restart or redeploy anything.

There's more...

Since LiveRebel is a complex and large subject (you can configure a lot of features), it cannot fit in this short book. For details about LiveRebel installation, configuration, and capabilities, please visit its online documentation. Also, you may find helpful information at `http://manuals.zeroturnaround.com/liverebel/index.html`.

Thank you for buying
Instant JRebel

About Packt Publishing

Packt, pronounced 'packed', published its first book "*Mastering phpMyAdmin for Effective MySQL Management*" in April 2004 and subsequently continued to specialize in publishing highly focused books on specific technologies and solutions.

Our books and publications share the experiences of your fellow IT professionals in adapting and customizing today's systems, applications, and frameworks. Our solution based books give you the knowledge and power to customize the software and technologies you're using to get the job done. Packt books are more specific and less general than the IT books you have seen in the past. Our unique business model allows us to bring you more focused information, giving you more of what you need to know, and less of what you don't.

Packt is a modern, yet unique publishing company, which focuses on producing quality, cutting-edge books for communities of developers, administrators, and newbies alike. For more information, please visit our website: www.packtpub.com.

Writing for Packt

We welcome all inquiries from people who are interested in authoring. Book proposals should be sent to author@packtpub.com. If your book idea is still at an early stage and you would like to discuss it first before writing a formal book proposal, contact us; one of our commissioning editors will get in touch with you.

We're not just looking for published authors; if you have strong technical skills but no writing experience, our experienced editors can help you develop a writing career, or simply get some additional reward for your expertise.

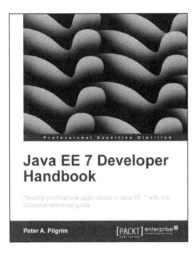

Java EE 7 Developer Handbook

Java EE 7 Developer Handbook

Develop professional applications in Java EE 7 with this essential reference guide

Peter A. Pilgrim

Java EE 7 Developer Handbook

ISBN: 978-1-84968-794-2   Paperback: 634 pages

Develop professional applications in Java EE 7 with this essential reference guide

1. Learn about local and remote service endpoints, containers, architecture, synchronous and asynchronous invocations, and remote communications in a concise reference

2. Understand the architecture of the Java EE platform and then apply the new Java EE 7 enhancements to benefit your own business-critical applications

3. Learn about integration test development on Java EE with Arquillian Framework and the Gradle build system

Java EE 6 Development with NetBeans 7

Develop professional enterprise Java EE applications quickly and easily with this popular IDE

David R. Heffelfinger

Java EE 6 Development with NetBeans 7

ISBN: 978-1-84951-270-1   Paperback: 392 pages

Develop professional enterprise Java EE applications quickly and easily with this popular IDE

1. Use features of the popular NetBeans IDE to accelerate development of Java EE applications

2. Develop JavaServer Pages (JSPs) to display both static and dynamic content in a web browser

3. Covers the latest versions of major Java EE APIs such as JSF 2.0, EJB 3.1, and JPA 2.0, and new additions to Java EE such as CDI and JAX-RS

Please check **www.PacktPub.com** for information on our titles

Java EE Development with Eclipse

ISBN: 978-1-78216-096-0   Paperback: 426 pages

Develop Java EE applications with Eclipse and commonly used technologies and frameworks

1. Each chapter includes an end-to-end sample application

2. Develop applications with some of the commonly used technologies using the project facets in Eclipse 3.7

3. Clear explanations enriched with the necessary screenshots

Java EE 6 with GlassFish 3 Application Server

ISBN: 978-1-84951-036-3   Paperback: 488 pages

A practical guide to install and configure the GlassFish 3 Application Server and develop Java EE 6 applications to be deployed to this server

1. Install and configure the GlassFish 3 Application Server and develop Java EE 6 applications to be deployed to this server

2. Specialize in all major Java EE 6 APIs, including new additions to the specification such as CDI and JAX-RS

3. Use GlassFish v3 application server and gain enterprise reliability and performance with less complexity

Please check **www.PacktPub.com** for information on our titles